PRIMARY SOURCES OF
FAMOUS PEOPLE IN AMERICAN HISTORY™

WILD BILL HICKOK

LEGEND OF THE WILD WEST

LARISSA PHILLIPS

rosen central
Primary Source™

The Rosen Publishing Group, Inc., New York

Published in 2004 by The Rosen Publishing Group, Inc.
29 East 21st Street, New York, NY 10010

Library of Congress Cataloging-in-Publication Data

Phillips, Larissa.
Wild Bill Hickok: legend of the Wild West/ by Larissa Phillips.— 1st ed.
    p. cm. — (Primary sources of famous people in American history)
Summary: Profiles the life and exploits of William Hickok, the legendary Western sharpshooter known as Wild Bill.
Includes bibliographical references and index.
ISBN 0-8239-4122-1 (library binding)
ISBN 0-8239-4194-9 (pbk.)
6-pack ISBN 0-8239-4321-6
1. Hickok, Wild Bill, 1837–1876—Juvenile literature. 2. Peace officers—West (U.S.)—Biography—Juvenile literature. 3. Frontier and pioneer life—West (U.S.)—Juvenile literature. 4. West (U.S.)—Biography—Juvenile literature. [1. Hickok, Wild Bill, 1837–1876. 2. Frontier and pioneer life—West (U.S.) 3. West (U.S.)—History—1860–1890.]
I. Title. II. Series.
F594.H62P48 2004
978'.02'092—dc21

                                                                2003005183

Manufactured in the United States of America

Photo credits: cover, pp. 5 (bottom), 11 (top) courtesy of Kansas State Historical Society; pp. 4, 19 (bottom) Library of Congress Geography and Map Division; p. 5 (top) courtesy of Larissa Phillips; pp. 7,15, 20, 28 Library of Congress Prints and Photographs Division; p. 8 Wilbur H. Siebert Collection, Archives of the Ohio Historical Society; pp. 9, 11 (bottom), 13 Library of Congress Rare Book and Special Collections Division; p. 10 © John Conrad/Corbis; pp. 12, 29 © Corbis; p. 14 Rare Book, Manuscript and Special Collections Library, Duke University; p. 17 courtesy of the Amon Carter Museum; p.19 (top) New-York Historical Society, New York, USA/The Bridgeman Art Library; pp. 21, 27 courtesy of Nebraska State Historical Society; p. 22 courtesy of Garst Museum; p. 23 © Hulton/Archive/Getty Images; p. 24 courtesy of South Dakota State Historical Society; p. 25 courtesy of Buffalo Bill Historical Center, Cody, WY.

Designer: Thomas Forget; Photo Researcher: Rebecca Anguin-Cohen

CONTENTS

1 THE BIRTH OF A SHARPSHOOTER

James Butler "Wild Bill" Hickok was born in Homer, Illinois, on May 27, 1837. He was the fifth child of William Alonzo Hickok and Polly Butler, a Vermont couple who married in 1829. The family moved west to Illinois in the 1830s.

This panoramic map of Homer, Illinois, was drawn in 1869 and is now housed at the U.S. Library of Congress in Washington, DC.

A descendant of the British Hickocks, William Alonzo Hickok, James Butler's father, was born in Vermont in 1801.

Polly Butler, a native of Bennington, Vermont, married William Alonzo Hickok in 1829. After living in the Northeast for several years, the couple headed west to Illinois.

The Hickok family members were pioneers who worked hard just to survive. They farmed and hunted for food. They made all their own clothes and furniture, and even their own soap. But they also helped runaway slaves escape. Helping slaves escape to safety was against the law.

THE UNDERGROUND RAILROAD

Slavery was legal in sections of the United States until 1865. Some Americans helped slaves escape. They hid them in their homes and then helped them sneak to the next house that would hide them. This network became known as the Underground Railroad.

UNITED STATES SLAVE TRADE.
1830.

This abolitionist print depicts the United States slave trade during the early nineteenth century.

At that time, slavery was legal in the United States. The Hickok family believed the law was wrong. These early experiences may have helped shape young James into the man he would become. Later known as Wild Bill, James Hickok is now one of the most famous men of the Wild West.

The barn seen in this photograph was a hiding place along the Underground Railroad.

This broadside, a woodcut image of a chained slave, helped illustrate the 1837 publication of John Greenleaf Whittier's poem "Our Countrymen in Chains," which recalled the horrors of slavery.

2 HEADING WEST

There are many legendary stories about Wild Bill. For a few years, he wandered from job to job, always heading farther west. One such story claims that a bear attacked him. When his gun was knocked from his hands, he wrestled the bear to the ground and killed it with a knife.

This photograph of Abilene, Kansas, *(above)* was taken about a decade after Hickok was appointed as a U.S. marshal for the pioneer district, a post created by Congress in 1789. Drawn to depict one of the many stories that circulated about Hickok's life, this illustration *(below)* appeared in 1867.

Another famous story claims that, in self-defense, Wild Bill was forced to kill nine men. Other people said that he killed only three men, and that he did it for fun. Perhaps that is when the name "Wild Bill" was born. Nobody knows for sure how a young pioneer became a sharpshooting legend of the Wild West.

Experiences that shaped Wild Bill's life were likely exaggerated. Today, historians aren't certain about many of them. It is for this reason that he is often referred to as a Wild West legend.

Wild Bill Hickok was the subject of several publications during his lifetime. This is the cover of the dime-store novel, *Wild Bill, the Indian Slayer*, which was one book that profiled his life in 1867.

3 ARRESTED!

When the Civil War started in 1861, Wild Bill fought to abolish slavery. Soon the Confederate army arrested him for his actions. The soldiers tied him up and put him in a shack that served as a jail. They told him he would be shot in the morning.

This 1889 drawing depicts the Battle of Gettysburg during the Civil War. Gettysburg, Pennsylvania, was the setting for one of the war's most decisive battles, fought July 1–3, 1863.

This 1863 photograph captured a group of Confederate soldiers in Charleston, South Carolina, during the Civil War. Around the same time, Hickok was reporting on Confederate movements from behind enemy lines.

Wild Bill's situation seemed grim, but a glint of metal caught his eye. It was a knife! He used it to cut the ropes around his wrists and to kill the guard. In a fury, he took the guard's clothes and escaped.

THE CIVIL WAR

The Civil War was fought between 1861 and 1865. The North, or Union side, wanted to end slavery. The South, or Confederate side, wanted to keep it. Thousands of American soldiers were killed. In the end, the North won and slavery was ended.

In 1867, while he was a U.S. marshal, Wild Bill Hickok was persuaded to sit for a formal portrait by the professional photographer E. E. Henry in Leavenworth, Kansas.

17

Two years after the Civil War ended in 1867, Wild Bill was appointed marshal, and then sheriff, of some of the roughest towns in Kansas. Then he was called to fight in the Indian wars. The settlers and the Indians were fighting over land.

THE INDIAN WARS PERIOD

The Indian wars were conflicts between the Native Americans, or Indians, and the U.S. Army, which was taking over their lands. This time in American history is known as the Indian wars period (1866–1890). The Indians had already been forced out of the East. Now the government wanted their lands to the west as well.

The lithograph *(above)* illustrates an artist's depiction of an attack on Native Americans at the Tippecanoe River, Indiana Territory, in 1811. This detail of a panoramic map *(below)* illustrates industrial developments in Kansas City, Missouri, around 1871.

MISSOURI RIVER

4 WILD BILL, THE SHOWMAN

During the Indian wars, Wild Bill acted as a guide and a dispatch rider for General George Custer. To avoid being killed by Native Americans, he disguised himself and traveled by night.

General George Armstrong Custer (1839–1876) in 1864. Although he had a prominent role in the Civil War, Custer is more often remembered for his fighting with Native Americans, such as in the Battle of the Little Bighorn.

Wild Bill's appearance in this photograph suggests that it was taken during his time as a showman (1872–1873).

By the end of the Indian wars, Wild Bill was famous. It was said that if someone threw a coin in the air, Wild Bill could shoot a hole in it. For a year, he starred in Buffalo Bill's Wild West show. But Wild Bill did not enjoy the life of a showman. He soon headed back to the real Wild West.

Wild Bill's lifestyle made him famous before he decided to become an actor. Besides touring in Buffalo Bill's Wild West Show, he starred in a play called *Scouts of the Prairies.*

This 1899 poster is an advertisement for Buffalo Bill's Wild West show.

5 THE DEATH OF A LEGEND

Wild Bill always said he would die with his boots on, and he was right. In 1876, Wild Bill headed for Deadwood, South Dakota, to mine for gold. Deadwood was a wild town, often plagued by barroom brawls that ended with gunshots. Wild Bill, who loved to gamble, felt right at home.

This photograph of Deadwood, South Dakota, was taken around the time of Hickok's arrival.

Wild Bill Hickok *(left)*, Texas Jack Omohundro *(center)*, and Buffalo Bill Cody *(right)* are featured in this photograph, which some historians have traced to the year 1873.

One afternoon in 1876, Wild Bill was playing poker in a place called Saloon Number 10. A man named John McCall arrived and shot him in the back of the head. The people in the saloon caught McCall and brought him to justice.

A LAST ROMANCE

In 1876, just five months before his death, Wild Bill married Agnes Lake Thatcher in Cheyenne, Wyoming. She was a well-known horsewoman who had run her own circus. She was often described as one of the world's first women to enter a cage of wild animals.

This is the last known photograph of Wild Bill Hickok, likely taken in 1875.

Today it's hard to know the truth about Wild Bill. He fought against slavery. But he also fought to push Native Americans off land that had been theirs for years and years. He claimed he had shot men only to defend himself, though others claimed he was a cold-blooded killer. It is certain, however, that Wild Bill was a true Western legend.

This sculpted headstone marks the grave site of James Butler Hickok. He was killed in 1876 by Jack McCall in Deadwood, South Dakota, where his body now lies.

Cowgirl Calamity Jane (Martha Jane Cannary) is seen here standing by Wild Bill's grave in Deadwood, South Dakota, during the 1880s. In 1903, Jane was buried next to Wild Bill.

TIMELINE

1837—On May 27, James Butler "Wild Bill" Hickok is born in Homer, Illinois, later named Troy Grove.

1856—Hickok leaves home for the Kansas Territory.

1861—Now known as Wild Bill, Hickok joins the Union army as the Civil War begins.

1862—Wild Bill serves in the Union army as a spy.

1867—Now working as a scout for the Seventh Cavalry during the 1867 Indian war, Hickok is appointed U.S. marshal.

1869—Wild Bill kills several men.

1873—Wild Bill stars in Buffalo Bill's Wild West show.

1876—Five months after his marriage to Agnes Lake Thatcher, Wild Bill is shot dead in a saloon.

GLOSSARY

abolitionist (a-buh-LIH-shun-ist) A person who worked to end slavery.

brawl (BRALL) A rough fight.

dispatch rider (DIS-pach RY-der) A soldier who carriers important messages from officer to officer.

frontier (frun-TEER) The edge of a settled country, where the wilderness begins.

legend (LEJ-uhnd) A person who has many stories told about him or her. Sometimes the stories may not be true.

outlaw (OWT-law) Someone who has broken the law and is on the run from the law.

pioneers (py-uh-NEERZ) Some of the first people to settle in a new area.

settlers (SET-lerz) People who move to a new land to live.

sharpshooter (SHARP-shoot-er) A person who is skilled at shooting.

WEB SITES

Due to the changing nature of Internet links, the Rosen Publishing Group, Inc., has developed an online list of Web sites related to the subject of this book. This site is updated regularly. Please use this link to access the list:

http://www.rosenlinks.com/fpah/wbhi

PRIMARY SOURCE IMAGE LIST

Page 5: These photographs of William Alonzo Hickok and Polly Butler Hickok were likely taken in the mid-1860s.

Page 7: This abolitionist print depicting slaves was found among the ruined remains of Anti-Slavery Hall in Philadelphia in 1838. It is now housed at the U.S. Library of Congress.

Page 8: A photograph of a farmhouse located in Painesville, Ohio, that was once a stop on the Underground Railroad.

Page 9: This broadside illustrated the 1837 publication of an abolitionist poem by John Greenleaf Whittier. It is now housed at the U.S. Library of Congress.

Page 11 (top): This photograph of Abilene, Kansas, dates from 1879.

Page 11 (bottom): An illustration of Wild Bill from *Harper's New Monthly Magazine*, which was first printed in 1867.

Page 13: *Wild Bill, the Indian Slayer* was a dime-store novel based on events in Wild Bill's life. This image is now housed in the U.S. Library of Congress.

Page 15: This 1863 Civil War photograph captured Confederate soldiers in Charleston, South Carolina, and is part of the collection of the U.S. Library of Congress.
Page 17: Wild Bill is pictured in this 1867 photograph taken by E. E. Henry in Leavenworth, Kansas. The Amon Carter Museum in Fort Worth, Texas, now owns the original plate.
Page 19 (top): This nineteenth-century lithograph, *Attack of Native Americans at the Tippecanoe River, Indiana Territory*, is housed at the New York Historical Society.
Page 19 (bottom): This detail of a panoramic map illustrates Kansas City, Missouri around 1871.
Page 20: General George Armstrong Custer is pictured in this drawing done by Alfred Rudolph Waud in 1864. It is now housed at the U.S. Library of Congress.
Page 21: This undated photograph of Wild Bill taken by Wilbur Blakeslee of Mendota, Illinois, was likely shot in the 1870s.
Page 23: This poster of Buffalo Bill's Wild West and Congress of Rough Riders of the World dates from 1899. It is now housed in the Prints and Photographs Division of the U.S. Library of Congress.
Page 24: This photograph of Deadwood, South Dakota, likely dates from the 1870s. It is now housed at the South Dakota State Historical Society.
Page 25: Hickok, Texas Jack Omohundro, and Buffalo Bill Cody are featured in this undated photograph likely taken around 1873.
Page 27: This 1875 photograph of Wild Bill Hickok is now housed at the Nebraska Historical Society in Lincoln, Nebraska.
Page 28: This photograph of the grave site of Wild Bill Hickok is housed at the U.S. Library of Congress.
Page 29: Cowgirl Calamity Jane is seen in this photograph taken in a Deadwood, South Dakota, cemetery during the 1880s.

INDEX

ABOUT THE AUTHOR

Larissa Phillips is a writer living in Brooklyn, New York.